I0412479

Negative
=
Positive

"Only If You Want"

FOR EVERY NEGATIVE SITUATION, THERE IS A

CHOICE TO TURN IT INTO SOMETHING POSITIVE

BY Michael John

authorHOUSE®

AuthorHouse™
1663 Liberty Drive
Bloomington, IN 47403
www.authorhouse.com
Phone: 1-800-839-8640

Published by AuthorHouse   03/05/2013

ISBN: 978-1-4685-0670-9 (sc)
ISBN: 978-1-4685-0669-3 (hc)
ISBN: 978-1-4685-0668-6 (e)

Library of Congress Control Number: 2011961392

Contents

This book is dedicated to my family and friends, who have provided motivation and encouragement for me to do what I love to do.

This book is also dedicated to anyone who has questioned who they are or should be in life, anyone who has tried to find themselves and is still lost. Hopefully, through my words, you can understand the meaning of being true to thyself.

ACKNOWLEDGMENT

I WOULD LIKE TO THANK, SWEET JESUS, AND ALL MY FAMILY AND FRIENDS. ALONG WITH MY GRANDFATHER WILLIAM THOROGOOD JR, DORA RICE AND MOST OF ALL MY IMMEDIATE FAMILY MEMBERS: MICHAEL RICE SR. (DAD) AUDREY RICE (MOM), MICKA RICE (SISTER), MALIK RICE (BROTHER), AND MARCUS RICE (BROTHER). YOU GUYS HAVE ALWAYS BEEN A CONSTANT SUPPORT, AND ALWAYS HAVE BEEN THE FUEL TO COMPLETING MY GOALS. TO MY PARENTS: THROUGH YOUR LOVE AND HARD WORK, YOU HAVE SHOWN ME HOW TO BE HARDWORKING

AND DEDICATED. YOU LEAD BY EXAMPLE WITH POISE AND CLASS. YOUR HARD WORK HAS PROVIDED US WITH CARE, SHELTER, AND LOVE. I AM TRULY THANKFUL. TO MY SIBLINGS: YOUR COMMITMENT AND ETHUSIASM MOTIVATED ME TO WRITE THIS BOOK. YOU ALL DO SO WELL IN EVERYTHING YOU DO. I APPRECIATE HAVING PEOPLE IN MY LIFE WHO UNDERSTAND THE RULES OF SUCCESS. YOU ALL ENCOURAGE ME, AND ALWAYS GIVE FEEDBACK, WHEN IT'S NOT AT ALL WHAT I MIGHT WANT TO HEAR. YOU ALL HAVE BEEN THERE FOR ME EMOTIONALLY, AND SPIRTUALLY. I LOVE YOU ALL SO MUCH.

MANY MORE PEOPLE HAVE INFLUENCED ME TO SET SAIL ON MY DREAMS. ALTHOUGH, I CANNOT NAME THEM ALL, HERE ARE A FEW PEOPLE I WOULD LIKE TO THANK: C. DICKERSON, KAREN HARRIS, NIA WILLIAMS, KRISTINA CONNERS, KESHIA LINTON, LATYIA WILLIAMS, DONNIECE BELL, LAURYN WASHINGTON. VANESSA LEWIS,

JASMIN WILLIAMS, LIBBY WILLIAMS, ERICA QUINTANA, LISA WARD, CHRISTINE HETLAND, JESSICA MILANI, CHERYL LEWIS, STEPHANIE BOROTA, STEFANIE MERRILL, LADONNA BOYD, DARNELL BELL, TAYLOR WING, MARK HAYES, CHARLES HARMON III, ALEX OCASIO, FRANK O, CHRIS MELBURN, BRADFORD POWNS, OTIS WILLIAMS JR., VERNON LAWS, DAVID TAYLOR, ALL SALT OF THE EARTH CHURCH MEMBERS, AND A HOST OF ALL OTHER FAMILY AND FRIENDS.

Yesterday's troubles shouldn't be carried over to tomorrow's worries because today wasn't even promised.

Every now and then, you may experience events that are unexplainable. These events usually occur when you carry over all of yesterday's problems into today and tomorrow. It may become so overbearing and stressful that you may be thinking of taking your own life. I have once felt this way, and I fully understand where your mind may be. To anyone who has lost a loved one to suicide, I wish I could have been there to offer advice, compassion, and most of all help. If you are considering suicide, the first step is to realize that there is help and that it's available for you 24 hours a day.

You can reach the 24-Hour National Suicide Prevention Lifeline at

1-800-273-TALK.

Negative = Positive

Always remember that it's perfectly normal to go through trying times, and you are just a human embarking on everyday challenges. You may have hit rock bottom, but you are not alone, and with courage and conviction, you can make it through whatever comes your way.

Michael John

In the beginning God created the heavens and the earth.

Genesis 1:1

Confused but Ready

(June 2006)

In the sorrows of every person there is a reason.

No one knows what's going to happen, when the wind

blows this season.

Everywhere you tend to go you're at a dead end,

With no options, no ways, no people, not a single friend.

You often reminisce about how life use to be, hoping you

can unlock the past,

But all you need is a key, which you just gave up on. Down

goes another task.

Hope and strength are the key to push past hopelessness,

But your mind is a powerful thing, giving you a guilty

conscience.

How far will you again go in this life? Will you go far

enough to fail?

Michael John

Will you ever reach the pinnacles where your life can
finally sail?
Could you ever be that person you imagined, thought, and
dreamed?
Or is it not made for you, not here, not even on a team?

Emotions flow, still can't explain how you feel, and no one
really knows.
You keep pushing forward, while you walk in circles, pain
down to your toes.
If someone can support you, you just might find your way.
You can be anything, get a lot for less, and never have to
pay.

The majority of your failure is mostly your own fault.
You have to get back up and go with what you were taught.
Life has ups, and life has downs,
Who is anyone to make a comment or dare try to put you
down?

Negative = Positive

Always inspire yourself to do the things they don't dare.

Become that shining star and watch as they all stare.

Life is what you make it. Shine bright and always go a little

too far.

Remember you were at the bottom.

You know where you've been and no one can define who

you are.

So when they all ask simply who you are trying to be,

smile, nod, and say, "My, oh my, I'm being simply me."

In the sorrows of every person there is a reason.

Now you know what the wind could possibly bring this

season.

One day to the next, they will come steady.

But this year, this summer, oh my you'll sure be ready.

—Michael John

Changes

(September 2008)

Again and again I replay in my mind,

Will I ever get past this time?

As the night came, and you wrapped up the day, questions

arose:

What would happen if it were my turn to die?

Who am I living for?

Do you think you can live another day?

How much can you endure?

Are you sure?

Or sure to let go, because if you can't continue,

you cannot stay, never to see another day.

Then you wake again tomorrow, faced with a little sorrow.

You realized you died last night, but yet you see the

morning light.

Michael John

Confused, hopeless, looking for who you are,

can't find the answers, realizing that you died

last night, you lost control and lost your mind.

Every day we should keep ourselves motivated,

others aren't always around to do so.

It's not their obligation to—it's truly yours to keep your

sanity.

When life isn't going well, you are the only person who is

obligated to change that.

We cannot depend on others to be our crutches, only to

handicap us further.

We need to make necessary changes to determine the

outcome of our lives.

—Michael John

"Father, forgive them, for they don't know what they're doing"
(Luke 23:34)

Reasoning

People ask, WHY? I answer back, WHY NOT? Why not inspire people of all ages by sharing my journey even if isn't the same generic story we're used to reading? Why not share my testimony if it could help millions or just one person? With so many negative influences in the world, why not dance, talk, sing, and write the things people need to hear to create happiness within them? My words are nothing but encouraging. They are meant to uplift others, those who are lost in the world and have no outlets. The ones who have no clear vision as to how to get where they are going, but see where they need to be.

Why not enlighten the world with the gift that has been blessed upon you? Why not, my brother? Why not, my sister? Why speak if it holds no true value? Why dream if it holds no passion and leads to no further planning? Why not inspire when it holds foundation, encouragement, and faith? We all have questions, but no one seems to have the answers. If they do have answers, they are often one-sided, and/or carry an ultimatum with a negative choice. So if you can give back, and inspire, why not? This is why I've decided to encourage instead of discourage. Uplift instead of looking down. Give long lasting words, not rated-R sounds.

Simply tell everyone out there that you do have a life. It's up to you to go through what is necessary, so you can begin to live. If I can change one person's viewpoint on how to live a happy life, by just encouraging them, by giving positive words, then why not? You don't have to have money. All you need is the gift of sharing, open arms, and a human heart. I'm writing this for people with self-esteem issues. People from broken families, who are tired, lonely, and at a point where they feel lost. People who are in their 30s who think life is over, people in their 40s who believe nothing else is obtainable. I'm writing this for people who don't know where to turn, people who are having a bad day, week, or year.

Mostly importantly, I'm writing this for people who struggle, and we all struggle and face seemingly insurmountable challenges. No matter what age, what race, this is for you.

Encouragement comes with no names on it. Your mind determines your stress level. Therefore, no one's struggles are greater than anyone else's, no matter what or where you come from. So if I can make you think a little bit differently than before, then I've accomplished my goal with this book. I believe, in life you must understand everyone's point of view, even if you don't agree with their actions. I understand!

My Actual Thoughts

In January 2010, I started to really look at my life as a whole. I had dropped out of college and was working three jobs. I wondered, is this how I wanted to spend the rest of my life? I wrote down all my pros and cons and wondered whether I'd ever be anything. Would I ever be that actor I wanted to be? Would I ever own my club? Would I ever get around to writing that book? Yes, I was having fun, working hard, making money, and having the time of my life. I bought a new car, but I was still really unhappy and in my corner, keeping to myself, just miserable. Some days I'd wake to find myself at a really low point, asking myself why I was so unhappy. I only felt this way because I wasn't really doing anything that I planned. I just came into a new year, and it felt like I needed to put so much behind me. I needed to become brave and embark on all the things I wanted to do in life.

Well, it wasn't easy, and it sure wasn't going to be a smooth ride. Trying to find YOU is the hardest thing you'll ever do. I thought for a long time about what I really wanted to do. I love to write so I decided to record my new journey toward becoming what I wanted to be. Writing is a powerful tool, and I encourage everyone to write down their thoughts day by day. Once you start and then one day go back and look at your first post and your last, you'll see so much growth, and so many more ways to grow. I wrote daily and I wrote down everything—every night was therapeutic for me. Still, I wasn't really fixing my problems as much as pushing them aside. So I decided to start a blog. As the journey began I wrote:

FRIDAY, JANUARY 29, 2010

The Introduction of Michael John

Welcome to my blog. Just wanted to give everyone insight into who I am. I'm just a hungry citizen trying to make a better life for myself. I'm not aiming to be famous, rich, or a superstar. I just want to be a successful young man. I'm originally from Chester, Pennsylvania. I now reside in New

Castle, Delaware, where life is anything but interesting. It's not really that bad, but with me coming from a city, and making my way here in the suburbs, you can only imagine how big of a change it is for me. Not until last year did I realize who I am or who I wanted to be. Lately, many opportunities have started to come my way. It's an exciting feeling. I'm a part of a non-profit organization called Deadline Production. Every day I talk with others and network. People who have gotten to know me have become a part of so many opportunities. I'm currently in the midst of writing a book, and planning to leave Delaware to move to Los Angeles, California. I'm inviting all of my family, friends, and everyone who's anyone to move with me through the days on my journey to becoming successful in completing my goals. You can follow me on Twitter at Twitter.com/MikeOJohn.

Here I was appearing so full of hope and energy, but really I was pushing everything that was bothering me aside. I was still in a lonely place trying to force myself to be happy, despite what my mind was telling me. Looking back, I realize how much in denial I was about my well-being and state of mind. I was lying to myself so I wouldn't have to face the facts! After I published my first blog post, I felt a tremendous high, and I knew I was going to do everything I said I'd do. Writing everything down made me feel powerful. Right then, I was whoever I wanted to be, fronting and putting on a mask. All for myself. It was just the beginning, and, boy, did I start off wrong, but I was thinking right! Sometimes we do this. We lie to ourselves so we can really believe something.

"I assure you, today you will be with me in paradise."
(Luke 23:43)

The Question and Reality

Have you ever dreamed of being who you've imagined, by doing what you want to do, how you want, when you want, and just being who you wanted to be? Yes, sometimes in our lives we've been at an all-time high, but we all know life throws us more than a few curve balls. Have you ever been at a very low point, rock bottom, and think you can't take anything else? You know, where you contemplating every move you make? Well, life isn't over yet, and it has nothing to do with what others think, but only what you think of yourself. Far too often, people spend years and years trying to find themselves instead of creating exactly who they want to be. When someone reaches rock bottom, it's always different from anyone else's rock bottom. Everyone is unique, and struggles vary. Too often, people think that rock bottom only pertains to financial matters, but nothing could be further from the truth. I often say that there are three stages until rock bottom. First you may experience a financial hardship and/or any hardship. Second, is the emotional state, where your become very emotional. Lastly, mentally you start to break down.

Sometimes it's hard to do anything you want simply because everything is going wrong in your life and you cannot see the light at the end of the tunnel. You need to realize there is always a way out. You hit road blocks when you plant them yourself. You may have hit rock bottom or may still be there. Please allow yourself some self observation to get back up, but only if you're serious enough to take it in fully. If you're reading this, do you dare challenge yourself to be better than you are and admit you're unhappy?

You can only change what you want to change when you realize who you truly are, and change is needed.

15 Questions

I had an opportunity to finish high school. I had an opportunity to go to college, and I had an opportunity to work. Through that, I used my opportunities, and because of that I am who I am. Now hard work is allowing doors to open. I know I am blessed, and I credit my parents, siblings, and mostly GOD. Many of us are blessed, but we also have to choose to take advantage of those blessings instead of taking them for granted. Did you have these opportunities? Did you take advantage? You ultimately control your life and the choices you make, even the little simple things in life.

1. Did you have the opportunity to get a high school education?
2. Did you apply for a job?
3. Do you push yourself?
4. Did you fail at something you strived to do?
   a. Did you try again?
5. Do you work hard for what you want?
6. Do you set goals?

a. Are you setting things in place to accomplish them?

7. Are you putting priorities first?

8. Are you living for you, by setting attainable goals?

Strive to be able to answer. "Yes" to the above questions.

9.   Are you blaming others for you hard times?

10. Are you using excuses to make a point?

11. Are you being lazy and/or procrastinating?

12. Are you dependant on others?

13. Are you trying to use people to get ahead?

14. Do you create hostile environments?

a. Are you quick to speak, and ignore often?

15. Are you putting fun before everything?

Your goal should be to answer, "No" to questions nine through fifteen.

"Dear woman, here is your son."
(John 19:26)

The Lie

There will come a time in life when you will no longer have to lie. At the end of the day you should be free to be the man or woman who possesses the confidence to admit your trials, tribulations, and mistakes. Often we don't know the full impact we have on people in our lives when we tell a lie. A lie can go on for a long time, which in the end turns into nothing. How many lies have you told that are still being believed? If you cannot come clean, or tell that certain person what you need to tell them, ask yourself who's in control. A lie is only as good as the person telling it. It's very dangerous to tell a lie, because lies destroy our credibility.

The point of telling a lie is to alter outcomes and gain time. Indeed the longer the lie, the longer the distrust and lack of forgiveness that will take place. If you find yourself lying often, you need to ask yourself what is your purpose or your reasoning. A man or woman who has to lie isn't at all what they need to be in life. You should be bold and speak your mind, realize and admit when you're wrong, and know that it's okay to make mistakes and not have to lie about them.

When you lie you may be hurting people—not just the person you lied to, but the people that person may come into contact with after they learn the truth. A lie sometimes spread to wide and too thin. Lies destroy credibility, relationships, and most of all trust. If you don't have your word, consanguinity, and/ or trust, you will have a hard time to thrive.

Finding Life

Your journey toward finding yourself and your life can be difficult. You really have to go and search out who you are. You have to realize that you can make your life whatever you want. At many points in our lives we question who we are and who and what we are we living for. Sometimes we just don't know who we are. We try and fit into places where we aren't meant to fit. Some people go through drastic life changes or experiment sexually to determine who they truly are. Try to change our view points, and opinions. We must learn that we are given choices in life. The choices we make determine the outcome of what we truly stand for.

We often make mistakes, but mistakes do not define our lives. They help mold us into better people. Making mistakes actually builds us up and helps us withstand more threats when we're trying to find ourselves. It's very hard to even imagine who we are when we've been who we are since birth. We have to think about life in a different way. We have to realize what is important in life and what it means to us. I was once on that path, because I was lost. I questioned my every move. I second-guessed every decision. There might come a time in your life when you believe you cannot and will not find yourself in life. You will tend to stay on a narrow path that leads nowhere. Ultimately, you'll be back at ground zero starting over, embarking on a journey that will bring you the same results time and again.

You can't find something that was never there. You are who you are, and you are human. You cannot ever find yourself in life, simply because life is something you create. You control who you are, you control what you want to do, and overall, you define who you are. To become truly who you need to be, you must create yourself and stop trying to find yourself. You must create yourself so that you can better yourself. Day to day you will face all types of challenges, but if you do not know who you are and where you stand, over and over you'll question key things about yourself. Above all, you should always be you, which is what you've created by the choices made.

"My God, my God, why have you abandoned me?"
(Mark 15:34)

My Actual Thoughts (Part Two)

WEDNESDAY, MARCH 31, 2010

"Thru My Eyes"

Another month down and more situations at hand. Sometimes life comes at you from all directions, and you might make decisions that may seemed right at the time and then realize later that they may have not been the best choice. You must know that you will change your mind, and you have to be okay with it. This month I've truly lost some things. A lot has happened, and I feel like I must share what's happened with all of my followers here. If nothing else, I need to write down my thoughts to get them off my mind. It's been a crazy month for me in terms of work, home, and relationships. It seems that I still couldn't find the corrective balance between the three. Working too much, but not wanting to; not being home to see my family, but needing to; and not having fun with friends, but wanting to.

Also, I lost someone greater this month. I lost myself, and just came to realize that I've been living my life but not in the way I wanted to. I'm not saying I want to go wild, but I can't remember the last time I honestly made a decision by myself without thinking about the reparations. When was the last time I relaxed and freed my mind? I truly can't remember, and I recently realized how my life has been going for the past few years.

The lesson learned "Thru My Eyes" is that you cannot live your life lying to yourself. For me working, working, and working more, was what I needed be doing . You can't live your life trying to make others happy. At the end of the day, you should not have to deal with your stress and the stress of others. You must do what you have to do to be happy. I'm not saying slay the world, but if you like doing it, do it! If you like jumping, JUMP! You may lose people for your own happiness when they don't agree with you, but at the end of the day you are only stuck with the decisions and actions you take. You must also take responsibility for those decisions. So why should anything else matter? "Thru My Eyes," you're the only one who controls your happiness!

When I wrote that blog post, I was a little further along with realizing some things, and I also knew I had learned a few things. Almost everyone in your life will have their opinions about whatever you are doing. This is why it's good to know that you can consider these opinions, but you don't have to act on every opinion. We have to take opinions for what they are, which is nothing more than someone's point of view about a specific situation. Opinions are formed from the knowledge and upbringing of one's true history. Therefore, to become who you are, you must learn to live for yourself. Create your life by doing what you want to do. While you create yourself, you'll get negative opinions from some people and positive ones from others. It's up to you to use your better judgment to determine what is right and what is wrong.

When I decided to let go of everything that was holding me back, I realized I simply could be who I wanted to be. Have you ever wondered why what you want to do is really out of reach? When you think further, do you replay in your mind what certain people in your life might think of you? Well, that's the first step in realizing that you aren't truly following your passion. We always should follow our instincts because that's how we live, love, and learn. We have to make decisions and stick with them. They may not be the right decisions, but we still learn from them. We make decisions so that we'll know which decisions not to make again.

In the Dark While Change Is Coming

January 2010

At times I'm all alone,

waiting and sitting in the dark.

I may be laughing and smiling,

but I'm not supposed to act lonely in this amazing park.

Laughing hides everything, by just showing teeth,

but it always comes back

and brings what underneath?

It's supposed to be good when you're home and asleep.

In the dark,

all by myself,

here alone.

Knowing it's bad for my health.

Doing everything,

just to keep myself busy.

Michael John

It's like I'm going in circles

and it's making me dizzy.

I may be in the dark.

Maybe it's where I need to be.

Yes, I'm alone.

Don't worry, it's just me.

But I believe, just like that man

who lives in the street and can barely stand.

You know, the one you call a bum.

But for me, unlike him, I know eventually, change is going

to come.

"I am thirsty."
(John 19:28)

Created Life

Here I am. After all the negativity and loss of friends, trying to keep a positive attitude. I decided to take my own advice and actually LIVE my life the way I wanted to live. First I wrote down all the things that were wrong in my life (ONCE AGAIN) and all the things I wanted to do. I thought about why was I so unhappy. I realized I didn't like any of my three jobs. I realized that people in high management jobs are more caught up in their egos than actually managing. It seemed to me that people were more worried about telling others what to do than boosting sales. I learned that there are so many negative and unhappy people in the world. I learned that people are hurt, angry, and miserable about their living situations.

Most important, I realized that I had let all these outside influences determine my mood, my attitude, my state of mind, my decisions, and, above all, who I was. I cared so much about other people's opinions and well-being that I forgot about myself. I forgot what it was to laugh, have fun, and live life. With these self-observations I began to create myself by going after everything I needed and wanted to go after. So I created myself. HOW? I started to live like I think everyone should live—by CONTROLLING my life. We can't let anyone determine our moods, our days, or anything about ourselves. We are the only ones accountable for our actions. I realized that I would one day grow old, and I don't want to die with regrets. So I decided to live day by day. Are you realizing some of these similar things? What will you do to create your life?

"It is finished!"
(John 19:30)

So Many Influences

Throughout life, becoming who you are can be difficult. Often, I go back and forth about what I should do and the things I should say or be. Faced with all these questions, I become confused about everything. For me it seems like if I do this or do that, somehow it might make me question my religion, my morals, my goals, and or just whether I'm being politically correct or not. I can't figure why I let all these other people's opinions and thoughts determine what I should do. I began to realize that you'll only be truly happy when you realize that amidst all these outside influences, it's up to you to pick which influence you're going to go by, or simply go with your own passion. Forget what someone may think of you or how someone may view you. It all comes down to how you want to live, and whether or not you are doing what is right. Once you have the perception, you should start leading. Once you have created life, you must always remember to give back. There is always someone behind you, doing the same things, using the same pathways, and making the same mistakes you've once made. Become a leader by simply giving that next person a helping hand. *You cannot gain nor grow, if you don't give back, and let go.* Simply, in life we should help people get to where we are, so we can go a step further. Therefore, always try and LEAD, by the example, never being the exception. To LEAD, you must *Learn* what is necessary, become knowledgeable, and confident in yourself. Be willing to **E**ducate others, and always remember to *Appreciate* appropriately, by giving good constructive advise. Lastly, remember to **D**elegate so that you don't think you have to do everything ourselves, which can lead to arrogance and the oversight of the talented people around us.

Learn . . . .

Educate . . . .

Appreciate.

Delegate . . . .

Lives are lost, people are gone. Hard to face that one day we will all mourn. Where should we go, what will we do? Another trail we must pull together, just to get through. Will we sing, or will we cry? Only trying to utter the word Goodbye. Hold on to faith, at a very slow pace, for we will get though it all, but at God's time and place.

Moving on is hard to do, it's what we need, only to get through. Through the pains, through the lies, no one knows how to cut all ties.

We can make it, especially when we know we can do anything.

Each day I can be greater than I was, knowing that no matter how bad the day started, I finished and got through it. I smile through rough times simply because I am highly blessed and favored.

*"Father, I entrust my spirit
into your hands!"
(Luke 23:46)*

Have I not commanded you?
Be strong and courageous. Do
not be frightened, and do not be
dismayed, for the Lord your God is
with you wherever you go. "
Joshua 1:9

The Result

At the end of the day we control everything around us simply by the choices we make. The choices we make determine where we will go in life. We must realize that choices are a part of everyday basic living. We cannot depend on others to make the decisions for our well being. When the end of the day comes, we are faced with the consequences that we have created for ourselves. We must again understand that not every decision that we make will have the desired outcome. However, we must learn from our mistakes as well as our successes.

When we go through things we often wonder whether or not it is our purpose to be here. I imagine that everyone has questioned their purpose and wondered if life is worth living. Mostly in trying times, when things unexplainable happen, we tend to think this. Getting over this hump is sometimes hard, but varies between the individual. When you're right in the mix of all of the lowest points in your life, you begin to drown in sorrow, worries, tears, and lack of determination.

The end result is that you are only feeling what you feel when you use all those things as crutches, support, and reasons why you cannot get past certain situations.

Know that if your think you're going to lose, you will. If you think you can't take it, you can't. Once you give yourself an option to fail, you will fail. Giving up may seem like an option, but it must not be. Even though through times you cannot see where you're going, it doesn't mean you're not going in the right direction. If everything is going great in your life, then something is entirely wrong. To be a better you in the end, you have to go through things to get further in life. At this point the things you once worried about, you won't worry about. The things you cried about, you will laugh about, and the things that cause sorrow, will be looked at with gratitude.

Through it all I can say that I have not lived long, compared to some but I have gone through trying times that seemed endless. Therefore, the question "How do you know that you're happy?" arrives, and all I can say is, when you don't have to lie about anything, you're happy and free. When you can talk about any situation you have gone through. Once you are delivered you are no longer attached to the negative.

I can say with pride that I am Michael John. That's it. I love my life, the direction its going, and overall the journey God has me on. Life is a journey, which is ever changing and forever challenging. Once you determine to stay true to your goals, passion, and God, no one will get in the way. So, after giving it your all, and trying to turn everything negative into positive. What happens at the end? You have to continue to ask God for understanding. There are things that doesn't require anything but prayer. Overall, in "The End" only you can determine the outcome of everything you go through. Are you going to let it kill you, break you, and/ or make you? Just because it seems that the negative has won, doesn't mean it has. Look at the things learned from the negative. They now have a positive impact on life, and you will realize that positive has always been the outcome in the long run. When you look around and it seems that love is lost remember that God is love.

Who Am I?

2012

I'm Michael John, 23 years old, an everyday person who can relate to your everyday struggles and situations. The person you can always come to in time of need. I'm here to tell you that you can refuse to be the person that people expect you to look like or act like. You don't have to be who "they" want you to be. I'm a motivator who supports others by trying to stay positive and caring. I'm a person who thrives on self-motivation and is very eager to encourage others through every avenue possible. I am a person who believes I have a responsibility to set an example of what life has to offer. I help others in any way I can, whether it be through words of encouragement or a helping hand.

I tend to take on a lot to keep myself busy, and it's not always easy to complete what I start. Right now, I'm a young man who is beginning to create life my way, by doing the things I'm passionate about. I am a person who lives knowing that mistakes will come up, and it's up to me to learn and to keep moving. I'm very outgoing, energetic, and happy about creating my life as I paint it. I am a brother, son, and friend, and I am very blessed to have the support system I have. I am a lover of all things that consist of fun. I am a person who understands everyone's point of view and is very good at offering unbiased advice.

I am who I want to be because I live by faith. Faith gives me the strength to carry out each and every day. You'll always find opposition in life, especially when you strive to be your best. I am who I am simply because I define my life, I define my world, and I define who I want to be. I am a person, a human, a citizen, and most importantly ME. I am fearless, encouraging, selfless, happy, changing, real, alive, crazy, fun, excited, full of energy, outrageous, giving, kind, caring, true, and, most importantly, I am MICHAEL JOHN.

MY FAMILY

MY PARENTS, SISTER, AND BROTHERS HAVE ALWAYS BEEN THERE FOR ME IN MANY WAYS. I COULD NEVER ASK FOR ANYTHING DIFFERENT, NOR WOULD I TRY TO CHANGE ANYTHING ABOUT THEM. MY FAMILY HAS ALWAYS BEEN POSITIVE OUTLETS ON MY LIFE, WHEN THE WORLD IS AT TIMES COLD. THROUGH THEM I LEARNED TO LIVE LIFE, BY GOING AFTER THE THINGS I LOVE, DOING WHAT I DREAMED, AND BEING ALL THAT I CAN BE. I WOULD LIKE TO SAY THANKS TO THEM AGAIN, ONLY BECAUSE THEY ARE THE DRIVING FORCE BEHIND ME. THEY ARE THE ONES WHO ENCOURAGE ME EVERYDAY WHEN IT SEEMS LIKE THERE IS NO HOPE. THEY ARE THE ONES WHO TAUGHT ME TO BE THE MAN I AM TODAY. MY PARENTS HAVE GUIDED ME EVERY STEP OF THE WAY, IN MY LIFE. THEY HAVE SACRIFICED SO MANY THINGS. I AM GRATFUL TO HAVE THE PARENTS THAT I HAVE. IN THIS

Michael John

LIFE IT SEEMS RARE TO HAVE PARENTS OF THIS
SORT. IT'S RARE TO EVEN HAVE PARENTS THAT
HAVE BEEN MARRIED AS LONG AS MY PARENTS,
BUT AT THE END, I LOVE THEM FOR NOT JUST
DOING IT FOR THEIR CHILDREN, BUT DOING IT
SIMPLY BECAUSE THEY WANTED TO. THEY LET
LOVE KEEP THEM CLOSE. THE SAYING NEGATIVE
= POSITIVE IS ONLY A MERE QUOTE THAT MY
FAMILY INSIPRED. WHEN I LOOK AT THEM, I SEE
THAT NO MATTER WHAT OBSTCLES THAT CAME
THEIR WAY THEY STAYED STRONG BY KEEPNG A
POSTIVE OUTLOOK, FOR THE PRESENT AND THE
FUTURE. IF I CAN GIVE BACK ANYTHING TO THEM
I WOULD GIVE THEM A THANK YOU. NOT ALWAYS
DO I SAY IT, BUT I AM VERY THANKFUL TO HAVE
THE SUPPORT SYSTEM I HAVE. NOT ALL HAVE
THIS BUT ALLTHAT IS NEEDED IS GOD.
AMEN

As I look back at my life for the past 23 years, I see trials I see mistakes, and most of all growth. I've learned that through it all I should always stay focused on what God has planned for me. Not everything has been easy, but I will not complain or hold anyone accountable. I learned to follow Jesus and stay true to myself. My LIFE, is not exactly picture perfect, but perfectly the way I pictured it, and it's GREAT. I am SIMPLY ME.

FOR EVERY NEGATIVE SITUATION, THERE IS A CHOICE TO TURN IT INTO SOMETHING POSITIVE.

FOR

NEGATIVE = POSITIVE

ONLY TRULY IF YOU WANT & BELIEVE IT TO BE

MICHAEL JOHN

The grace of our Lord Jesus Christ be with you all. Amen.

Revelation 22:21

The Quotes

By : Me (Michael John)

Read Three Daily, and Think about how it reflects to you:

"Many times we take life for granted, not knowing what tomorrow will bring, so each day we shall try to tell those who we love that we love them. If we can, we should hold on to the good memories and everything should be okay. Still, every now and then we are faced with sorrow."

"Sometimes in life it's best to move on and get over things. Why hold on to something that over time turns into nothing?"

"Every day I see what I want to be but don't know how to get there. Every day brings a new challenge I'm faced with. One day, one mountain, all handled one day at a time. So as I steadily climb the mountain we call life, I know there isn't a limit to what I can do, or where I can go. I must climb to the top until I die and reach the top, what we call heaven."

"You've been going at it for years now, still undecided which way to turn. One path leads this way, the other leads that way. Where do you go? You must move forward."

"Remember that what goes up must come down. Life has its ups and downs. So why act surprised when something bad happens?"

"We may all at one point Begin to Hurt, and we need an Urgent Rescue so we can again Triumph again, and again!"

"Life is more than color or race. Humanity is far more important than color of skin."

"Don't worry about who I used to be. Just worry about who and where I'm trying to be."

"In life you will lose things—friends and even family. You go through trying situations because they help you to be content with yourself. You must understand that you have to make mistakes so that you'll make fewer mistakes."

"Every day should bring something different. If you see yourself in an everlasting non-changing day, it's time to change something. Change is good and often the best path to take."

"In life you may struggle, be stressed, and even hit rock bottom, but you must use the rocks to build, use them for protection, and shelter. Even though you may fall again, it won't be as hard as the first time. Life is about learning. You can't learn without living."

"Never let anyone tell you that you're too old—or too young—to do things. Life has no time stamp, and having faith has no limits. Only you control your life. You decide what you care about and where you want and need to go."

"Funny how people avoid you, and then, in later years, after learning about your success, they flock to you like flies on a hot summer day."

"When you have come so far from where you were in your past, you might think there isn't any place left to go—until you see your past creeping up on you. You must keep pushing on so your past won't become your present again. You must learn to keep striving until you are stable, content, and comfortable."

Negative = Positive

"Sometimes our anxiety to do certain things causes unwanted mistakes; we must indeed slow down, evaluate, and proceed with caution. It's not best to rush into anything without fully understanding what you may sign up for."

"We all struggle in life. Although we come from different backgrounds, it doesn't mean one struggle is greater than the other. We all go through trying times. Just because one is rich and one is poor doesn't mean struggle and hard times don't occur equally."

"When family acts up, we sometimes hold them to a higher standard. We must remember they are human like everyone else. Still, you may have to cut them off for a short period. This may hurt, but holding on may be hurting you far more than you think."

"Sometimes it's best to cut family off for a little while, especially when you don't have the support that's needed. Sometimes families use failures, insecurities, and jealousy to fuel their thoughts and opinions, which translate into less than great advice. Cutting family off isn't a bad thing; you will use glue every now and then to patch up things in your life."

"The day isn't done until your work is done. Your work isn't done until the day is over, and it isn't over 'til the fat lady sings. There aren't any fat ladies in my vision, and they won't be appearing anytime soon."

"Moving forward is sometimes hard to do, but you can't get where you need to go by standing still and settling."

"You can't stop and stare at your dream. You have to run fast, so that in your sight it becomes bigger and bigger until you can reach out and grab it."

"You must remember that life moves on, so if you decide to stand still don't be surprised when one day you wake up and you're old, dusty, and with a mouthful of wishes. You must move with life to have a good time."

"Don't worry about the mistakes you make when you're on the road to success. Just don't forget what they were and remember to stay focused."

"Doing what you want is the greatest feeling in the world. Don't let anyone take your happiness away. If you want to do it, and enjoy doing it, do it however many times you like."

"When you're not doing what you want to do, life gets boring, and you may become angry. You must fight and make your own decisions. It's a part of growing up."

"When you really don't want to do certain things, and you're really not sure what to do, and everyone else offers pros and cons, lean to God for better judgment."

"Sometimes it's best to take a break so you can learn to appreciate things a bit better—things such as relationships, work, family, and friends. When your break is over you'll feel better and eager to continue."

"Go with your gut. It always knows when you're full of shit."

"Often, people take us for granted, and sometimes we let them. You must take charge and remove these people. They will only do what you allow them. Don't settle for anything less than you have to. Don't become a victim of someone else's insecurities. It welcomes un-needed stress."

"Goals you may want to accomplish may seem so far away. Patience, dedication, and determination will get you to where you need to be. The trials and tribulations along the way teach us how to get through struggles. Once you reach your goals, you're ready to keep going no matter what obstacles might come your way."

"You may want things you don't need, but you must focus on the things that are needed so in time you can do and get the things you want."

"Your work isn't done until you decide to give up. Every day you'll be faced with giving up. It's up to you to suck it up and continue to move past negativity."

"At the end of the day you should always feel confident to wake up tomorrow. Coming home to great family, great TV, and a great bed is something to look forward to. Don't let a stressful day stop you from enjoying the small things in life."

"Every now and then you'll go through pain. It's the only way to gain strength and grow. You must get past and over it, because pushing it aside will only have a greater impact later on."

"The very same people doubting you will be the very same people that make you motivate yourself to do what you love to do, even when the odds are against you."

"Thinking you have to maintain an imaginary front is wrong. Remember that pretenses always turns colors, breaks down, and burns all too quickly. Being real prepares you for everything, because nothing can be thrown at you, especially when you didn't fake it."

"When everything is going badly, something should always take over and not only tell you but show you how really good you have it."

"You can never know what the outcome of change is if you never try."

"When you're almost done, remember that for each task completed, for each phase in life, there are always new challenges and work to get done."

"When you're in a tough position, it's always best to look to God for purpose, understanding, and guidance. No matter what the decision is, it's guaranteed to be the right one."

"Just when you think you're in a jam, God shows you the peanut butter and now you're ready and prepared."

"To be you is being unique. Trying to be someone else is, well, just dumb. If you don't love yourself you're simply living."

"When giving all that you can give, and nothing seems to come of it, you might drift into space, into nothingness. You'll slowly lose sight of who you are. CHANGE IT!"

"You must understand that you can only be the person you want to be when you let go of all the strings holding you back."

"When trying to find yourself, and you can't. Just began creating yourself."

"Always encourage your friends to do better and offer them words of encouragement. Never try to buy your friends. In life, words can buy you more than money can. Money may buy and build houses, but words buy and build character and long lasting relationships. Money is exchangeable; friends aren't."

"Never take life for granted. Always tell those who you love that you love them. You may control yourself through the actions you take, but you cannot control your last breath. So always live life like you're living your last moments, because one day they will arrive."

"Some of your best memories and moments will be at the cost of your greatest failures. This tells us we're in control of our own happiness."

"In life we must all make decisions for ourselves, and we must make them no matter the consequences. It's a part of growing up and a part of creating our lives."

"When life seems to be going fast, take a step back, look at the situation, and evaluate the things that went wrong."

"At the end of the day, in every situation, true colors, real friends, and real faces will ALWAYS show, no matter what mask or makeup covers them. Facades (or Masks or Pretenses) always fade to reveal the people behind them."

"When things stress you out, lean to God, for He's the only one with answers to all your insecurities, even the ones you deny to yourself."

"Attraction might catch my attention, but you'll need substance to grab my focus. In the end, looks fade. You shouldn't want someone just to look at, but also to hold a conversation with."

"Once you stop setting goals, you stop living. You must learn always to go a step further than where you are, even if you have a million dollars."

"Give all that you can give, so in the end you can live life the way you want to. Along the way you will make mistakes, but it's all a part of growing as a person."

"In the midst of all troubles, Jesus is the only one who can guide you until you're sure. He doesn't offer second-guessing or criticism. He knows what's best even when we think we know it all."

"Every day you have a chance to be better than you were yesterday. It just takes one extra step to go further."

"Sometimes, you have to give a situation time. You'll have to step back and postpone your decisions, opinions, and conclusions. You'll never know how much time is needed until it happens. Be patient."

"If you have a dream, make it reality so that you have no dreams but actualities."

"Embrace who you are, because being you is the best thing God has given you. And you are truly one of a kind."

"If someone disrespects you, you should address it immediately, nip things in the bud so they won't reoccur. If you don't, the situation will likely become worse. There's nothing wrong with telling people how you feel in a respectful manner."

"Life becomes fuzzy and unclear when you decide to let go of the wheel. Always be independent, and be the driver of your life. No one should drive you to do anything. Be new, be you, and above all be self-driven."

"Having 'good' friends doesn't even come close to having a great family."

"Sometimes we put things aside. Sometimes we keep doing so, and we never accomplish our goals. You should always live your life—you only have one. Are you living your life for you?"

"Why let the slightest things alter your family bonds and relationships? You need to get it together. Fix it because you cannot change everything, and one day it may be too late."

"Family is something God has given to us, to share, to live with, and create long lasting memories."

"Yesterday's troubles shouldn't be carried over to tomorrow's worries, because today wasn't promised."

"If everything is going well in your life, you should ask yourself what you are doing wrong."

"Don't be impatient or rush things. Everything is worth waiting for, especially when you wait a long time and nothing happens. Then it will happen, unexpectedly, but on time."

"The grass isn't always green, but that doesn't mean you can't change it. Every new change comes with new challenges."

"If you wake up to see another day, there isn't any reason why you should wake up on the wrong side of the bed."

"If you've gone through abuse of any sort, you might tell yourself that it's not that bad and/or that it's your fault. You must dig deep to fight for something that the abuser didn't give you, and that's life."

"Depression is nothing more than you telling yourself that you can't overcome your current situation. You must beat it by learning that struggles are a part of life and you can overcome anything that comes your way."

"We were all born for a purpose. It's why God has given us life. It's up to you to find what your gift is and use that gift to maintain your purpose."

"We may not agree with some people's actions, but we must understand their actions. For every action, there is reason, and for every reason there is a purpose."

"You have to love to live life, and live so you can love life."

"Remember that we all have to go through hard times so we can go where we need to go. You may hate your current situation, but you must love the fact that you can learn from this situation and prevent it from happening again."

"Never let anyone make you feel negatively about yourself. If you like who you are, just be that. In the end, no one can live your life, and no one is responsible for paying your debts but you."

"Facing the facts is sometimes hard to do, but you have to face the fact that you must move past some things to get to other places."

"At the breaking point, realize that destiny will always be the outcome."

"Every day should be great, especially knowing that you're one day past everything negative that happened yesterday. Be new, and most importantly be you."

"Love life and it will love you back."

"When you're faced with challenges and can't figure out which door to knock on, be very patient and wait for a knock on your door. Things are within reach only when you make yourself reachable."

"People can't fix something they know nothing about. Always explain with reason so you won't be bitter to a person who knows nothing about the situation—one that he or she might help you fix."

"Going one step backwards to research, evaluate, and learn from your mistakes is much more productive than going three steps further unprepared and not knowing the possibilities that could arise."

"Push yourself to the limits, aim for space. You'll reach the stars and learn to love. You'll be loved and learn to give, and you'll always get something back. Most importantly, stay true. That way, no one can ever take you away from being you."

"When you think you're done, nine times out of ten you're not. It's always best to reevaluate before proceeding. You should always be sure so you won't be sorry."

"To be perfect is to be at a standstill, with nothing more to learn, and no more growth. Always strive to be perfect, because you'll always learn and grow."

"Self-esteem only has to do with YOU, and only you control it."

"Choices and decisions always have to be made, even if not wanted, so that you can grow in life."

"Why worry about what others say, when those people don't know the true meaning of how words really impact people?"

"At the end of the day, who shall be responsible for all your actions but you?"

"If you think you can change the world, realize, that change doesn't mean permanence. It means evolution and growth."

"When you believe that you're in control, you can do anything without anything to start from."

"Life comes with its ups and downs, but ultimately only you determine if you come out on top."

"Don't get too excited and comfortable when first meeting someone. Everything isn't always what it seems."

"Sometimes it's best to evaluate your life as a whole, correct what needs to be corrected, and move on."

"Tough love molds the soul, little or big. There is not one word too big, or too long, to change a heart."

"You can't compare your life to another's when you haven't walked in their shoes. One struggle isn't greater than another just because you were raised differently or come from different backgrounds or different places. Struggles come from the ability to cope, or not to cope, with what your mind is telling you."

"Understanding the true nature of why people do things is how we know that some people are misguided and only react the way they do because of how they were raised. Help by simply understanding their reasoning, by educating with rationality and guidance."

"Life is what you intend it to be, so why should anyone else change it? If you need to move on, do so. Never become content with misery."

"For every problem there is a solution, and you must understand that the best solution may not always have good outcomes but still is indeed the right one."

"Each day something or someone will discourage you directly or indirectly. Self-empowerment and your will to push through negativity will help you succeed and reach positive results."

"When you give you shall receive. No matter what you give out you'll always get back, good and bad."

"Sometimes there is no need to speak up, but you must at some point draw a line and speak up so people know that respect is given only when they give it."

"Most of what holds us back from our dreams comes from fear. Once you overcome fear, you are guided with the best thing God has given you: FAITH."

"If they tell you that you can't, show them you can. If they tell you that you won't, tell them you will and then how. Never let anyone discourage you from doing positive things in your life. Simply live."

"Being angry and mad is sometimes an excuse used to avoid expressing how you feel. Always be truthful and say how you feel so you can be at ease with yourself."

"Your courage to go through rough times shows that worldly things cannot break or change you."

"You'll only begin to move forward once you've realized why you were pulled back."

"You are in complete control over your mood. No one is to blame for your feelings but yourself. Never let anyone get you up or down, especially if you don't want to be."

"In the awakening of happiness there will always be sadness. It's up to you to change that around. In the awakening of sadness there will always be happiness."

"You should never contemplate whether or not you need to be treated with respect, no matter the situation. Respect is mandatory, never optional."

"Every day, your mind will challenge you to contemplate your commitment and strength to fight through adversity. It's strictly up to you to overcome adversity by simply believing in yourself."

"Every now and then we will be faced with sorrow. Just know that God will not put anything on you that you cannot bear. Everything happens when it is supposed to."

"Being patient is key; you will never know what God's plan is if you can't wait it out."

"Never be scared to go for anything. Fear kills dreams, while actions make dreams a reality."

"Some of the best advice for yourself is often the very same advice you've given others."

"No matter what, at the end of the day, always count on yourself to be your true motivation. It's all you truly have."

"Many situations may be unfortunate, but they aren't unfixable. Learn, move on, and ultimately grow. Make mistakes, and you will gain wisdom. Make excuses, and you'll lose integrity."

"For each day there is a new opportunity to be greater than you were yesterday, and a new opportunity to be thankful."

"Money isn't everything. Some of your best moments and memories occurred when you didn't have as much as you have now."

"In the midst of challenges, there may be laughs, tears, and pain. To get you through, always remember where you were and how far you've come."

"The measurement of a man is only calculated by the number of decisions he's made, and the ownership afterward, even if they were mostly mistakes."

"In life you need discipline and motivation. When you lack discipline, motivation will guide you, and when you lack motivation, discipline will lead you."

"Giving up is only an option. Don't discourage yourself by letting challenges cloud your judgment."

"If you have doubt for any reason, shoot straight for the root, not the breakable branches."

"For every negative situation, problem, or position, there is always a choice to turn it into something positive."

"Success is only determined by how bad you want it, and how far you're willing to go to get there."

"When something good ends, remember there is always an opportunity for a new and better beginning."

Michael John

"Through it all, if you can look back and realize the mistakes, the trials, and triumphs, it was all worth it. Everyday will be challenging, but without obstacles you can't grow."

"It's always good to appreciate those who mean much to you. Be thankful that you mean much to God, who died and arose for our mistakes and our sins!"

DURNING THE BOOK, and AFTER THE BOOK!

I Am? That's All

(2011)

When I first walked in the door, you probably started to

judge me.

So why Am I standing up here, trying to convince you who

I am

Because If I am what you thought when you prejudge,

when I walk through the door

I'm nothing more, than the thoughts of your mind.

You see, I can be a lot of things, But I chose not to be those

things

Simply because I define me. And If I am who I say I am,

Then I need to be up hear explaining who I am, expressing

my feelings, and telling you who I Am

See, remember you already prejudged me when I walked

through the door, or maybe when I sat down, or when I first

spoke, maybe now as I am speaking

Michael John

See I am not the average person that you may think. I am
Michael John.
Michael John, Michael John? Who is he? Who may he
be? Coming up here telling me how I thought, and what I
thought of him?
But again you need to know this is who I Am. My name is
Michael John.
I am just a man trying to make it in this cold world,
growing up just like you
I may not have been through the things you been through,
But I understand, and I know it's a
Real, real, cold world out here, and to make it you have to
strive real hard, and try to never look back, and somehow
keep moving forward when you're attacked.
And it's kind of hard to express myself to you, because you
don't know me, but oh yeah you judge me
And Here I am, trying to be firm and Clear, When I tell you
my name is Michael John most don't even come near.
For now that all you need to know, because I f I try to
convince you anymore, I may turn your head,

Negative = Positive

And now you're looking at me sideways. And I can't make
you understand where I've been or who I am.
So with this, this is exactly who I am, my name is Michael
John,
Who tries to be no one but me? So when you see me do me
a favor, and do not judge me
Because my name is Michael John and I here to stay, no
matter what you thought about me, I'm going to do me
I'm going to strive and go forward, Keep on pushing past
the past, and moving forward '
Again and Again I'll push forward, Forward, and forward
again I go, and I'm going to keep on saying it to you all
know, that simply I'm Michael John, and that's the way it
goes.
I am me not you that's all you need to know. I'm me not
you, I'm me not you, I'm me not you. I am Michael John
winter, spring, summer, and fall. HELL, I stand tall, never
changing who I AM, THAT'S ALL

Stereotypical/Analytical

(2012)

Why should I walk and talk like you

Why should I be all the things I am not?

Simply because you want me to be the stereotypical,

analytical human persona

Of what it is to be "In." Well to me that a sin,

To pretend to be whom I am not. Simply because it hot.

NOT, I will not be eased in, or eased out. Just because I

will not shout, that

I am something you want me to be. I know I don't fit in the

box, but again, I don't have to stop

Simply because I'm doing the things I want to do. No

stopping anytime just to impress you.

Wait pause let me tie my shoe. So I can take this journey.

The journey where you ask

I thought you wanted me to do as you ask.

Now you want to know all my business, trying to be my

friend.

Well, to me that's like a sin,

to pretend you actually like me, and then turn you back on

me spitefully.

I know you lack in education, simply if you thought I'll

give you all what you've been chasing. My Mind, My

Body, My soul, and my heart.

Stop playing, no one get that, not even when I surrounded

by dark.

So please keep moving because your nothing but the

stereotypical analytical creature made of fakeness.

Only comes around to get the juiciness, and then when I'm

suck out, and dry, your fast away, SHOO little fly. Only to

repeat the cycle again and again,

Well to me that's a sin.

To use, abuse, and go to the next,

so this time I may be the Stereotypical, analytical human

persona, and tell you all that you want to hear.

Than when it's all said and done, and it's the break of

dawn,

I will fly out cause you were just my pawn.

Negative = Positive

I sit you down and tell you how I once had a friend and all

they did, well was sin.

And they trapped me. So I wonder why I should be all the

things I am not, why.

Simply because I am not the stereotypical, analytical

human persona made of a lie.